C000148133

About this booklet and how to use it

Looking at the advert opposite might fill your eyes with tears of laughter, or make you wince at how close to the truth it is. We so easily find our identity in how we look. The right hair product, make-up, shoes will prove to the world that we're "worth it".

This booklet aims to help women think through the theme of *identity*: what it is, where we look for it, and what God says about it. As part of that we'll be taking the time to read parts of the Bible, especially Psalm 139.

You may think: *"What has an ancient book got to tell me about being a woman in the 21st century?"*

The answer is that it has a huge amount to say: because the Bible is the word of the one who created us in his own image - God himself.

As we listen to what God tells us about himself and ourselves, we'll discover the true source of our identity in the one who came to rescue us.

A word about what else is in here. This booklet is designed to be done once a day for 19 days – roughly three weeks (allowing for a couple of those how-did-it-suddenly-get-so-busy days!).

PLEASE NOTE:

1. Truth and change take time. Try to work through the book one day at a time, rather than get through it in one go! This will allow you proper time to reflect on what you've been reading, and see how it can be put into practice in your life.

2. Understanding truth and making changes requires discipline. In many cases we will be battling against ingrained habits and wrong thinking.

3. Thinking right, and real change, require God's help. We simply cannot do it by ourselves. We need God's Holy Spirit to work in us to change us. So as you read and think, ask God to help you believe and act on the things he shows you.

Most days you'll be reading a part of the Bible, thinking about some questions, and working out how it applies to your own situation. Other days, you'll read an article on a particular issue, or a story by someone who has struggled with how they see their identity.

One of the ways God helps us to change is to make us part of a group of people who face the same issues. So it would be great to meet up with some other women if you can, perhaps from the church you attend. As you do the studies on your own, and then get together to discuss them, you'll be able to encourage each other to trust in God's goodness and find your identity in him.

exploring identity © Naomi Skull / The Good Book Company 2011
Published by The Good Book Company, Elm House, 37 Elm Road, New Malden, Surrey, KT3 3HB. www.thegoodbook.co.uk
Unless otherwise indicated, all Bible quotations are taken from the New International Version (NIV).
Design by Jon Bradley. Printed in the UK. ISBN: 9781908317575

known

Have you ever felt life would be so much easier if you were better understood?

I remember vividly the teenage feeling that your parents don't really know you, know nothing about your likes and dislikes, don't understand your worries or how you should be treated.

Even now I sometimes wish my closest friends could know me better, understand how I could feel more loved by them, understand how things they have said have hurt me.

And family life would be so much simpler if my husband read my mind, or my children automatically understood what I ask of them.

"Why am I like this?"

There are also times when I don't know myself. I don't understand why I react in certain ways. Why do some things make me cry on some days and not on others. Some days all I can see is red, and some days all I feel is blue. Even as I write this I'm thinking: "Is this just me? Does anyone else feel like this?"

And that's the nub of it: we all have moments of real isolation, feeling that nobody knows us or understands us, that we don't belong or fit in; feeling like some kind of freak; imagining that everyone must think we're idiotic.

"Why does no one like me?"

These doubts play on our minds and haunt us. On a free day with no plans, my daughter asked me who we were going to see so I texted round a few friends. Everyone else was busy.

Instead of thinking: "That's nice. I hope they're all having a lovely day with other people," I immediately felt insecure. Why had no one wanted to see me? Why hadn't anyone checked if I was free? Did I really have any friends if they were all so busy seeing each other?

Irrational, maybe! But these feelings of isolation and self-doubt often rear their ugly heads, and with damaging results.

"If only I could be more like..."

Friendships turn into comparison games. Instead of loving and feeling happy for our friends, we get jealous that they have better looks or are funnier or more popular. We become consumed with what other people think of us; and that determines what we wear, how we act, and what we say.

Even our acts of kindness and friendship are spoiled by our selfish desire to be needed and loved more than anything else. We end up wearing a mask: not the true me, but the me that I want everyone else to see, designed to cover up the deficiencies in my character.

But then I wonder why no one really knows or understands me... and so it goes on!

Psalm 139 v 1-6

1 O LORD, you have searched me
and you know me.

2 You know when I sit and when I rise;
you perceive my thoughts from afar.

3 You discern my going out and my lying
down; you are familiar with all my ways.

4 Before a word is on my tongue
you know it completely, O LORD.

5 You hem me in—behind and before;
you have laid your hand upon me.

6 Such knowledge is too wonderful for
me, too lofty for me to attain.

"If only there were someone..."

We're all stuck in a vicious cycle - longing to be truly known and understood, and yet hiding our real identity from those around us to make ourselves seem acceptable. If only we could have the security of being completely known and understood by someone...

Known

All my worries about my identity...
• come from being shaped by what other people think of me.
• leave me feeling inadequate.
• mean that I hide parts of me from other people.

And yet, *I am known.*

God's knowledge of me is intimate. He has a closeness to me that no one else has. He knows all of my movements: when I'm in or out; when I'm sleeping or watching TV; on a bad hair day, or any bad day. He knows my thoughts; what is more – he understands my thoughts! Even I don't understand them sometimes! *I am known.*

Questions for discussion

• From these verses, what exactly does God know about you?

• How does that make you feel?

• Is there anything surprising about the amount he knows about you?

• What do you find out about God in these verses? Does that change how you feel about him?

what is identity?

Before we go any further, let's just think about what we mean by "identity".

It's not just the information given on your passport; it's about who you actually are... What makes you tick? What makes you happy, or sad, or angry? How do you define yourself? What's important to you?

Those are the things that influence your behaviour, emotions, and priorities, including, most importantly, where Jesus fits in.

Where does Jesus fit in?

You see, for most of us, even Christians, when we dig deeper into the depths of who we are, we'll discover that Jesus is not where we find our identity. He's usually slotted in somewhere between Sunday morning and evening, and perhaps once more in the week. We might happily sing about him being the "King of kings" and our "All in all", but how often do we include him, let alone bow to him, in everyday life?

Sadly, we can be more influenced by the world around us... defined by what the media says is important... too busy trying to make our lives look neat and respectable... rather than letting the King rule.

The following questions are intimate, but hopefully show how we shape our identity and what's most important to us. It will help to be honest and open about these things as we think about identity, and to be willing to do some hard work thinking about who you are.

Time for some soul searching

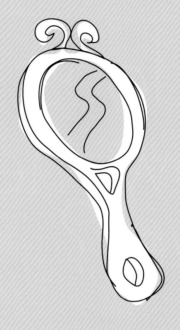

- How would you describe yourself? Maybe start by just choosing three words.

- How do you think people around you might describe you? What would they see as most important in your life?

- What do you like others to see in you?

- What do you keep hidden from others? What do you fear people finding out about you?

- What has the biggest influence in your life? Fashion? Media? Friends? Parents?

- What do you feel you need from other people in your life?

- How do you compare yourself to others – do you feel inferior or superior?

Sadly we are more influenced by the world around us, defined by what the media says is important

The starting point

However, as you look back on the first six verses of Psalm 139 (see page 3), who is the main focus? It's God, isn't it? It's all about what he knows.

This is so not how we think! In our society the individual comes first – my needs and rights above anyone or anything else. So discovering who I am is all about "looking inside myself" to find "the real me".

But that is not the way of the Bible. What God knows about us is what is important. Verse 6 tells us that this knowledge will blow our minds! We are better known by God than we can possibly know ourselves, and that is what we are going to uncover.

STEP

3

why does he know me so well?

In the beginning...

The creation story - you probably know it already. But just step outside of creation for a minute and imagine yourself as a spectator. The canvas is blank, dark and empty. There's nervous expectation as you wait for the greatest artist ever to take centre stage.

Then, lights! Finally, someone has turned the lights on and we can get this party started! Already it's looking better, but hang on – it's all just water. Is that all this creation is going to be?

No, here we go... there's something separating the water, a huge space appearing above... the sky! Well, who would've thought of that! It works well though, doesn't it?

The greatest artist ever ... centre stage

Now we've got water and sky – what's coming next? A darkness seems to be emerging from the water, and all the water is moving to one side. This patch is becoming dry... it's land! Well, what a fitting contrast. So we've got sky, sea and land. But it could do with some more colour.

But wait, the land is changing: it's turning all different colours. Things appear to be growing: tall things, short things, fat things, round, green, pink, – a multitude of colours.

Wow, these must be plants, fruit, trees. They give such vibrancy and colour. The land looks so rich. So full.

I must say the sky is beginning to look a bit dull now.

He's thought of that too! Before the words are out of my mouth, lights appear. A big one in the day, a smaller one at night, and thousands of tiny, beautiful, sparkly ones all across the sky. It's awesome to look at. Now everything is ready for... life!

Life! In the sea, in the air – everywhere teeming with life! Moving, breathing, flying, swimming. A beautiful array of colour and shape and movement – and noise! Imagine the noise as all these newly-formed birds find their voices for the first time!

But it doesn't stop there. There's still more life... on land. The diversity, the scale, the wonder, as species after species is created.

Crawling, hopping, walking, trotting. Beaks, snouts, antlers, tails, trunks, horns, manes. Could you have come up with so many different varieties? From the gigantic to the microscopic, the blueprints are all here and the canvas is full.

Or is it? There is still one creation to watch, but this one is different.

All this is just the backdrop to God's greatest masterpiece...

Read Genesis 1 v 26 – 2 v 7 and 2 v 15-25

Questions for reflection

• How is the creation of mankind different from the creation of the rest of the world?

• What added details are there?

• What do these details tell us about God's knowledge of us? How well does he know us?

*t*estimony   HELEN'S STORY

As a child I often dominated parties and gatherings with my bubbly, loud, sometimes annoying personality.

Even when I became a Christian at 19, I'd not learned to calm down – which made for some interesting, giggle-filled prayer meetings!

But at 24 I did change. Maybe I was calming down and growing up... but then why the tears? You expect those from a teenager, but not someone in their early 20s! Something wasn't quite right.

It wasn't that I woke up one morning and felt down. But I gradually realised I couldn't remember when I last enjoyed myself. I started to avoid people and social gatherings. When asked how I was, I'd say: "Fine", then quickly change the subject.

How could I tell them I'd spent the night before crying so much I'd given myself a nosebleed? That wasn't me. It wasn't the bubbly, lively person they thought I was. I felt ashamed. It felt as if someone had changed me without my permission, and I didn't know why.

I didn't want to admit it, but depression had sneaked up and taken over. I hid how I felt and avoided situations that might force me to open up and confront my feelings. My battle with sin was almost non-existent and my relationship with God became business-like and impersonal. I felt angry and abandoned by him. Didn't he care about me any more?

Months passed and the tears turned into numbness. Finally I told a friend how I felt. I was frustrated that I couldn't give a reason for my feelings; I was just depressed. We kept meeting and reading the Bible together. I knew what I was reading was true, but it had little impact on how I felt. My feelings told me I wasn't worth anything to God, or anyone, while I was like this...

After a "good" year, I now believe the reason I went through depression was to make me realise how loved I am by God. Ok, I was relieved when the depression lifted, but it was more than just relief. It was only on the other side of my illness that I could see how good God had been to me.

Even in the darkest depths, he hadn't let me slip from his hand. He'd been there looking after me. It was me who pushed God away... he hadn't abandoned me at all!

God didn't need me to be the exciting, bubbly person I thought I was. He didn't need me to be anything. Even before the world began, God knew this would happen. He knew I'd react badly and push him away... and yet he still loved me, enough to send Jesus to die on the cross for me.

A love like this wouldn't disappear because I wasn't "chirpy" any more. He'd love me whether I was the life of the party or a blubbering mess in the corner!

The truth is, no matter what I go through, God is there with me

He'd taken away the thing I thought made people love me – to show me that he loved me without it. God had changed me, without my permission, but for my good... it had just taken me a while to see that.

On days when life is tough, and the tears start, a little bit of me panics. Has it come back? Will I have to endure that suffering again? But the panic quickly subsides and reality kicks in.

The truth is, no matter what I go through, God is there with me. His love doesn't depend on me, but simply on what he has done through his Son, Jesus.

STEP
4

We always used to argue on a Sunday morning.

Sundays meant church all morning and then visitors for lunch. An endless – and unrealistic – list of tasks filled my head: hoover... clean the bathroom... cook... tidy up... sort the dishwasher... lay the table... All of it needed doing before our guests arrived.

Why? So they'd see how well-ordered and tidy we were. But how to get all these things done? Invariably I'd end up incredibly stressed: invariably my husband would suffer!

Does that sound familiar? Do you frantically clean up when someone is coming over? Especially if it's your mother-in-law?! Maybe some of us even avoid inviting people into our homes because we don't think they're up to scratch.

Our hidden selves

Now, there's nothing wrong with a bit of cleaning, but why do I stress about it? Perhaps it's all about giving people a picture of my home – and me! – that's different from the reality. I try to hide the messy bits. But while I might be able to do that with my house, can I do it with my heart?

What messy bits of your life do you try and hide from others? Your struggles with work, children, or sexuality – do you bury them all beneath a cool and calm exterior identity? Your shyness and sense of worthlessness – do you mask them with extreme fashion styles and behaviour?

That feeling that no one could love the real you – do you throw yourself into helping others to show how much you are needed?

The hidden cost

Often people suffer with brokenness and struggles that they think are unique to them.

are you hiding?

They feel they're the only ones who can't cope, while everyone else seems fine...

It's simply not true! We all struggle, we all try and hide things about ourselves that we don't want others to see. I desperately want to be recognised for the things I can do, not the things I can't do.

This sense of hiding ourselves comes across very strongly in the psalm, but who are we hiding from?

Psalm 139 v 7-12

7 Where can I go from your Spirit?
Where can I flee from your presence?

8 If I go up to the heavens, you are there;
if I make my bed in the depths, you are there.

9 If I rise on the wings of the dawn,
if I settle on the far side of the sea,

10 even there your hand will guide me,
your right hand will hold me fast.

11 If I say, "Surely the darkness will hide me
and the light become night around me,"

12 even the darkness will not be dark to you;
the night will shine like the day,
for darkness is as light to you.

- What lengths does the writer imagine going to in trying to hide from God?

- What does he find?

- What do we learn about the character of God?

- What's the bad news here? What's the good news?

- How do you try and hide from God?

Wouldn't we all love to hide the bad bits of ourselves from God – to make him think we're much better than we truly are? So when you read this, it's scary; it makes you gulp. "So he knows everything?!"

The bad news is...

All our cover-ups are a waste of time. Ok, so we might be able to hide what we're really like from some people... sometimes! But if "darkness is as light" to God, what does that mean for the dark depths of our hearts? The shameful memories, the guilty secrets and the thoughts we refuse to own up to – God sees them all!

The good news is...

We can stop hiding who we are from God. Even our worst deeds, our most evil thoughts don't surprise him. He'll never say: "Well, I never knew you were that bad!" Our darkness is just like light to him; he knows who we really are, warts and all.

The question is...

Can God sort out our mess? Can he know us as we really are, and still accept us? Can he turn our darkness into light as well?

If yes, then here's the answer to our struggles with identity. We can come to God, without pretending, or putting on a mask, or first doing the impossible – trying to tidy up the mess of our hearts ourselves.

He already knows you – could that be good news for you?

Read John 3 v 20-21

- Who likes to hide and why?

- What solution is hinted at here?

STEP 5

God doesn't make mistakes

D oes my bum look big in this?

Can any of us honestly look in the mirror and say, hand on heart without a hint of doubt: "I praise you because I am wonderfully and fearfully made"? Or do we secretly think: "I wish my nose was smaller... my stomach flatter... my thighs firmer..."?

Ok, maybe your thighs aren't the problem, but you'd be hard pushed to find a woman who is 100% happy with her looks.

View from the pew

And isn't this just the biggest area where we play the comparison game?

In church, as your friends walk in, what are your immediate thoughts? *"That dress looks amazing on her – I wonder where it's from?" "Why do I never look good in that colour?" "Oooooh, nice bracelet!"*

Have you ever realised how perverse those thoughts are? You're in church – you're meant to be worshipping God. Yet you're consumed with image, fashion, clothes! Hello?!

Why are our looks so important to us? Partly because in our culture how you look is exactly how you're judged. Your clothes speak volumes about who you are, how much money you have, who you like to hang out with – we dress like the people we like.

Comparative crisis

And we're bombarded daily with images of perfectly honed bodies... flawless skin... smudge-free make-up... straight, white teeth...

Imagine a poster model with unshaved armpits and spinach stuck in her teeth – it would make a rubbish ad, but we'd all feel much better about ourselves!

Instead, advertising images leave us feeling inferior and ugly. So few of us can truthfully say we are wonderful creations, because – just look at us! Comparatively speaking, we're not a pretty sight!

Psalm 139 v 13-16

13 For you created my inmost being; you knit me together in my mother's womb.

14 I praise you because I am fearfully and wonderfully made; your works are wonderful, I know that full well.

15 My frame was not hidden from you when I was made in the secret place.
When I was woven together in the depths of the earth,

16 your eyes saw my unformed body.
All the days ordained for me were written in your book before one of them came to be.

- What images does the writer use to describe how we are made? How does that add to what we've learned already?
- What more does this say about God's knowledge of us?
- What does it say about our appearance and personality?

Confessions of a guilty knitter

I'm not a granny, but I love knitting – it may not be the coolest hobby, but, hey, my kids have warm clothes!

I love the imagery here of God knitting us together. I can just imagine him with huge needles, deciding where each strand of DNA goes.

Every single stitch shows on a piece of knitting – giving shape, beauty and individuality. And that's exactly how God created us each individually.

The Master weaver

He was involved in creating every aspect of our physique and personality – intricately, intimately, precisely. God made our inmost being, gave us our character, likes and dislikes – loud or quiet... into heavy metal or classical music.

It's God who knit us together fearfully and wonderfully... wove together our frames... saw us in our unformed state and made us up exactly to the design that he wanted – the shape of our noses, the colour of our eyes and the speed of our metabolism.

And what do we find out about God's work? It's wonderful! There aren't any mistakes! God knew how your body would be affected by genetic inheritance, scars and ageing. He set your body on its course. Nothing that's happened to you is unexpected to him. He has a purpose in everything he has decreed for you.

God's masterpiece

Have you ever climbed a mountain or seen a breathtaking sunset and thought: "Isn't God's creation amazing!"? But this psalm says that looking in a mirror should take our breath away! Remember, all of creation is just a backdrop to God's masterpiece – humans, me, you!

Or gross monstrosity?

The message women get from the world around us is: too fat; too thin; your boobs aren't big enough; your legs aren't slim enough; you should be blonde, you should be brunette – you're NOT GOOD ENOUGH!

RUBBISH!!! That's not what God says. You were made without any mistakes, fearfully and wonderfully. So, who are you going to listen to?

"I felt that not having children eroded my identity as a woman"

Caroline never found out why she and her husband couldn't have children. They tried everything – every medication and doctor available – but fell into the 1% of people who never find a reason for infertility.

How much of a woman's identity do you feel is tied up in being able to have children?

So much! Not only is there pressure from culture, friends, family, all asking if you're thinking of starting a family – but also, as a woman, you have that natural desire to have children.

The Lord has put that desire in your heart. It's a pressure we feel from the Bible too. Genesis 1 v 28 says to be fruitful, fill the earth and subdue it.

How did you feel to have that part of your identity as a woman withheld from you?

You can easily allow yourself to feel worthless. After all, this is what women were created to do! And of course there are times when you have to deal with all different feelings: resentment,

jealousy, asking God: "Why me?"

I was also angry at myself for desiring something that was not meant for me. Infertility can take over your whole life and become the only issue that you focus on if you let it.

For me, every month and every period was another loss, another time to grieve. It was a wound that would never heal, and regularly opened up when I least expected it.

How did you cope with those feelings of worthlessness?

Only God can put the healing balm on that open wound. It can be an incredibly lonely path, especially the older you get, as more of your friends start families.

But you have to make sure the Lord walks that path with you; this isn't something you can deal with in your own strength.

Each step we took I had to keep coming back to the Lord as my rock and refuge, and stand on his promises in the Bible. Zephaniah 3 v 17 says: "The LORD your God is with you, he is mighty to save. He will take great delight in you, he will quiet you with his love, he will rejoice over you with singing."

Verses like this tell us the truth about God and his good character, but also how he feels about us.

> For me, every month was another loss, another time to grieve

This wasn't the Lord punishing me or withholding from me (though I did have to work through those issues at different times). This was the Lord teaching me that his ways are best – better than my ways. That doesn't stop him from delighting in us.

It did eat away at my identity, it did hurt, but there was always hope and that trust that I had loving arms holding me up.

You talked about grief. What was the grieving process you had to go through?

There were times when I begged the Lord to take away that desire for children that he's put in a woman's heart from the beginning of time. He did not.

The grief is something no one else can really understand, but I used to read a lot about Hannah (1 Samuel 1) and how she would pour her heart out to the Lord in grief – so much so that Eli thought she was drunk!

That was actually a good model for me. I would allow myself to cry and to grieve, but again to come back to those promises – it's not that the Lord doesn't love me.

I think you mustn't underestimate that need to grieve when you are disappointed month after month, but you must also ask the Lord to help you get the balance between wallowing in pity and genuine grieving.

What advice would you give to someone going through the same struggles that you had?

You have to guard your heart because you can let so much creep in. Facing situations such as visiting new babies, I had to pray for the Lord to help me through.

One thing I did was surround myself with godly friends who I could be completely honest with and say: "This is rubbish, I don't understand it."

They would be there to pray with me or cry with me when I was tempted to despair because it was so easy to be weighed down when left to my own thoughts. I'm so thankful for those friends, and for the promises in the Bible that God kept reminding me of and bringing me back to.

I would also recommend that, however painful and awkward it may be, you let the people close to you know about your struggle. Educate people, be honest with them – not every detail, of course, but enough so they can be sensitive and praying for you, too.

As you reflect, what do you think are the big lessons God was teaching you about your identity as a woman?

It would have been so easy to let this become the main thing, to let it dominate my life and my marriage. I had to come to terms with the different plan the Lord had for my life.

But when I look at the big picture, and who I truly am, I can only find my identity when I am cocooned in the Lord, not in whether or not I'm able to bear children.

The Lord did have children prepared for me. We were able to adopt two beautiful children who were fearfully and wonderfully made especially for our arms.

It was a long and painful process, and at times I didn't understand at all what God was doing. But he is the one who knit me together; he knows every iota of my being, so who better to trust with the big picture of my life. He is the only place where I can find hope, value, worth and identity.

> *I can only find my identity when I am cocooned in the Lord, not in whether I can bear children*

mankind makes a mess

Theres a reason why all of us inevitably struggle with who we are and who we want to be.

There was a time when humans weren't worried about what others thought of them...

Before the fall

Genesis 2 v 25 says: *"The man and his wife were both naked, and they felt no shame."* Wandering around a beautiful garden in your birthday suit is probably not what you'd associate with feeling no shame. And yet that was how things were before "the fall" (human rebellion against God and its consequences). Adam and Eve didn't need to be embarrassed about nakedness. They were happy with who they were and how God had made them. Shame didn't exist! No hiding, no need to put on a front, no confusion over identity, no need to prove yourself. But it didn't take long for the lies to filter in...

Read Genesis 3 v 1-19
- How does the serpent begin to sow seeds of doubt in Eve's mind?
- Go back to 2 v 16-17. Has Eve got all her facts straight? Why not?
- What's the picture of God that the serpent paints for Eve?
- How similar is your view of God?
- Does that picture match what we've seen of God so far in Genesis and Psalm 139?
- How does eating the forbidden fruit affect Adam and Eve's relationship with God? And with each other?

Other voices

Shame, fear, hiding, blaming – it all starts here. The serpent took the truth and twisted it just a little and just enough to make Eve doubt her Creator. *"He's not interested in your good. He's been lying to you. He doesn't really care about you."*

Can you hear the echoes of the world around us in those phrases? *"You're not really* unique and precious, you're not created with care, you're not loveable and you're not loved." Maybe it's all a little too familiar... and all intended to make us doubt our Creator.

Wrong choices

Eve was sucked in. Why? Because she saw something she wanted.

It would be easy to label Eve as the victim here, but she wanted what the serpent promised: she wanted to be like God. Ignoring her God-given identity – fearfully and wonderfully made to rule over all creation under God's care and commands – she chose instead to disobey the One who knew her best.

And, hey, we would've done the same. How do I know? Because daily, constantly, we imitate Eve. Listening to lies about who we are, believing them and doubting God's truth.

Then, to top it all, trying to carve out an identity for ourselves in our looks, achievements, status and personality.

Adam and Eve were the blueprint for all humanity, not just physically, but also in nature. Were you or I in that garden, our hearts would have gone after the same thing. We too are hungry to be the gods of our lives.

Consequences

The results of the fall are devastating. Adam and Eve have previously enjoyed God's company in the garden; now they hide from him, scared of being found out. Ring any bells?

Psalm 139 v 11-12

11 If I say, "Surely the darkness will hide me and the light become night around me,"

12 even the darkness will not be dark to you; the night will shine like the day, for darkness is as light to you.

Their intimate relationship with God is shattered – not because God has changed, but because they are ashamed.

And it's not just their relationship with God that's broken. Adam and Eve immediately embark on the first ever marital spat, and it's not a pretty sight! They both want to shift responsibility from themselves and point the finger elsewhere.

Look again at Genesis 3 v 1-21.
- How are the results of the fall seen in your life (especially in your struggles with identity and relationships with others)?
- What do verses 15 and 21 show about God's character?

Why does God say: "Your *desire* will be for your husband, and he will rule over you"?

"Desire" (v 16) doesn't mean women swooning in a dribbling heap every time their husband walks into the room. Rather, it means that the wife will desire to take the husband's place.

The big temptation for women is wanting to be in charge – wearing the trousers, whether married or not. However, in families God has given leadership to husbands and in the church to men. God's curse means that this gets to us women because we believe we could do better than men!

Men generally find their sense of worth in work and achievement; for women it's generally in who they are and what they can control.

In verses 17-18, God frustrates the plans and desires of both sexes to make us realise our continual need of him. He wants us to turn to him in dependence and trust, not to continue in our rebellion, confident in our own efforts.

turning heads

As we've seen, Adam and Eve were the first to hide from God. Eve's head was turned by the delicious-looking fruit, which reputedly would also offer her wisdom like God's.

Eve wanted to be like God. Who could resist? The fact that God had forbidden it went out of her head. Here was something that looked good and promised to deliver a better identity. So she did as she pleased and took it. All humans have followed in Eve's footsteps ever since...

Read Romans 1 v 21-25
- What is it that humans do and don't do?
- Why does this happen?
- What is the result?

Idol lies

Mankind's problem is rooted in this great exchange – the truth for a lie. And the lie is that created things can give us what we need.

That's how we end up worshipping stuff. An idol isn't only a bronze figure sitting in a shrine. Our idols may be very ordinary things – things that we think will give a flattering impression of who we are.

What is it that turns your head? What makes you do a double take, and sigh wistfully: "If only..."? Is it big beautifully decorated houses? Designer clothes and bags? Romantic relationships? Happy families?

Car-struck

Perhaps, like me, it's fast cars. I confess that I once dated a guy purely because of the car he drove. Shallow, I know.

But for me, a car says so much about my identity. There are some cars I wouldn't touch with a bargepole! And when I'm choosing a car, the name on the badge will always win over practical things like fuel economy.

Here's a small window into my heart. Just a simple thing like buying a car highlights the emphasis I put on image and identity over everything else.

Sadly, I'm duped into believing that a lump of metal, rubber and plastic will give me the satisfaction and happiness that I crave, shaping me into the person I want to be.

Possession obsession

- What do you daydream about?
- What are you really living for?
- What is it that drives you?
- Take a look at the receipts shoved in the back of your wallet. What window into your heart do they provide?

Shiny new things promise much, but deliver very little. How long is it before the shine fades? A week? A month? Surely none of us are still boasting over a new purchase a year later?

But possessions are only part of the picture. Where else are you seeking an impressive identity? What other things may be your idol? One of the most revealing questions is: What disaster do I most fear?

How does God feel about idols?

In the book of Hosea there's a brutally honest illustration of how God views our attempts to find our identity not in him but in other things. God's prophet, Hosea, is told to go and find himself a wife – but not just any ordinary wife...

Hosea 1 v 2-3 (ESV)

2 When the LORD first spoke through Hosea, the LORD said to Hosea, "Go take to yourself a wife of whoredom and have children of whoredom, for the land commits great whoredom by forsaking the LORD."
3 So he went and took Gomer, the daughter of Diblaim, and she conceived and bore him a son.

Exchanging the truth of God for the lie that idols can give us the identity we want is like prostituting ourselves.

In creating us intricately and intimately, God has given us a wonderful identity. But we reject it for a cheap, shoddy, repulsive replacement that may promise much, but cannot deliver.

Right now, why not ask God to rescue you from the idols you have identified in your life?

Exchanging the truth of God for idols is like prostituting ourselves

Identifying our idols

Timothy Keller, in his book, *Counterfeit Gods*, suggests some other questions to help us identify things that have become our idols:

- What triggers your uncontrollable emotions – fear, anger, stress?
- Where do you desire to have control?
- What happens when you experience huge change in your life?
- How do you respond to unanswered prayer?

Have a look at the following areas.

Marriage:
Is the thought of being single horrifying to you? Are you getting on with life or waiting for a husband? Do you find security and worth in being attractive to the opposite sex? Do you sometimes fantasise about having a different husband?

Family:
Do you find security and worth in being needed by your spouse, children or other relatives? If you're a mother, how do you feel about your children growing up and leaving home? How do you feel when other families seem to be functioning better than yours?

Friendships:
Do you find security in knowing that you have lots of friends? Would you describe yourself as a people-pleaser? Do you need to be needed by others?

Status:
Do you need to be recognised for what you are doing? Do you get grumpy when you are not given important jobs?

Blending in:
Do you just want to be left alone? Do you find security in hiding yourself away from others?

Standing out:
Do you need to be noticed? Seen as quirky... edgy... unique? Do you hate to be defined like everybody else?

*t*estimony

Gomer's Story

Even though I know I'm safe now, sometimes I still wake up in the middle of the night shaken by my own frightened screams and covered in a cold sweat and tears. I always have the same recurring nightmare – and it terrifies me.

In the dream, I'm back in the marketplace being sold as a slave. I'm not worth much any more. I've lost the beauty of my youth. My lover, who promised me so much, no longer wants me and for a good price I know he'll hand me over to anyone.

I was never his wife, never his treasure, only a temporary possession he could throw away when he was done. I've tried pleading with him, but it's too late – he's already replaced me with another woman, just as I once replaced the one before me.

A crowd gathers, shouting insults, calling me dreadful names. Men grab and touch me, they have no respect. They wouldn't treat their mothers, wives or daughters like this – but I'm nothing to them.

I even see men I've slept with. I don't remember their names, but I know them and can tell by the look in their eyes they won't help. I'm not the same body they once adored. Now I'm old, ugly, worthless.

I think my only hope is if I'm lucky and Baal shows me kindness. I might be bought as a slave and have enough to eat, but I know I won't be loved; I'll be used, beaten and raped.

Then I see Hosea, my first love and my husband, the only man who wanted me to have his name, share his life and be the father of all my children. I was so young back then; I thought I wanted more than just to be his wife.

Flirting with other men turned into compliments, which became kisses and before I knew it I was sneaking out of the house. It was exciting, passionate and dangerous. I loved the attention and compliments – they told me I was beautiful, so that's how I felt.

As Hosea walks nearer, I notice his hair is greyer than before; it's years since I walked out on him. I'm ashamed and hope he doesn't recognise me.

I was never his wife, never his treasure, only a temporary possession.

Then someone behind me shouts: "Hosea, remember Gomer? Here's your wife the whore, who's slept with half the town". The crowd roars. I'm the only one not laughing.

Hosea is a godly man. Even when I first met him he was telling everyone not to worship Baal and to worship only Yahweh.

So it's no surprise that when he pushes to the front of the crowd to take a closer look, he begins to recite his holy teaching and in a loud voice says: "If a man commits adultery with the wife of his neighbour, both the adulterer and the adulteress shall surely be put to death".

The crowd cheers and he picks up a large stone and throws it at me, shouting: "Gomer, you are a whore".

Like most nightmares, I always wake up before the stone hits me and I die. Normally I'm thrashing around in the bed, trying to shield myself from the stone, calling out to Hosea. The nightmare always ends this way – and leaves me terrified and shaken.

My husband is used to my nightmares, so in the night he gently caresses and kisses me, stroking my forehead to calm me. As I cling to him, he whispers again and again that he loves me and that I am safe in his arms.

Who is this wonderful new man in my life, you may wonder. He's not a new husband. This man with his arms wrapped around my aging scarred body is my first love, my only husband, my Hosea.

It still amazes me. That day in the marketplace he didn't stone me, he didn't come to mock me as I deserved.

Instead – years after I'd broken his heart, broken our wedding vows and destroyed my reputation – he was not filled with righteous anger, but with love and forgiveness.

Hosea had heard I was being sold at the market and he came with the intention of buying me back. I was bought for a good price, neither to be his slave nor to be beaten, but again as his wife.

He loves me and he remembers my past no more. I am proud to be his wife.

Based on the Old Testament book of Hosea

Jesus –
everything we're not

Hopefully by now you're thinking through some areas in which you're tempted to find identity and value. But there's that huge problem, isn't there?

The more we think about the way in which we have "prostituted" ourselves to our idols, the more we want to hide those things from God. Digging out some of these rotten things just makes us want to bury them again and pretend they're not there.

So how can we get from here (knowing the darkest depths of our idolatry and identity-seeking) to where the writer of Psalm 139 is (comfortable with God knowing everything about us)?

Let's reflect on someone else's identity...

Read Colossians 1 v 15-20
This passage is like Jesus' CV: it gives us his credentials, gifts and status.
- •What things do you learn about Jesus' identity from this passage?
  It might help to put some of those things into your own words.
- • How does God feel about Jesus?

Ultimate identity
What a glorious picture of Jesus – our Creator... Sustainer... Ruler... Protector... and Owner! He reveals God to us; he is the beginning and the end; and in everything he is ultimate. So what is his ultimate purpose? These verses tell us: reconciliation, peace, blood.

Ultimate purpose
Jesus uses his unique, ultimate identity for us... To make idolatrous "prostitutes" like us acceptable to God. To make ungrateful, self-centred rebels like us friends with God. To make it ok for guilty, shame-stricken humans like us to be known by God.

But this had to be done through his death, through the spilling of his blood, through the shameful humiliation of the cross.

Ultimate event
So it was no ordinary man who died on the cross. Jesus was, and is, the God-man.

The same man who commands the earth to revolve around the sun, the forces of gravity to hold the universe together and the intricate laws of nature to nourish life on our planet, also allowed blood to pump through the veins of those banging nails into his hands and feet.

He was sustaining their life as they took his away. Why? For us.

Look at John 12 v 44-46
- • What more do you learn of Jesus' identity and purpose here?
- • What one thing is required of us?
- • Look back at Psalm 139 v 11-12. How do Jesus' words here develop the thoughts of the psalm-writer?
- • How should Jesus' words help us overcome our fear of God's intimate knowledge of us?

Jesus longs for us to stop hiding ourselves from God. He's come to reveal God to us, and to bring us into the light. It was, and is, his passion.

- • How will you respond to him right now?

what Jesus knew

Having our idolatrous hearts exposed is a painful process. So what happened when Jesus, the light of the world, met people like us with dark hearts?

Let's look at some of these encounters, recorded in the Gospels. We'll see Jesus meeting people, and dealing with them compassionately and graciously, even though he fully knows the idols in their hearts.

What happened when Jesus met people like us with dark hearts?

Read Luke 10 v 38-42
- What were Martha's priorities? What idol does that point to?
- How does Jesus deal with her?

Pray: If you recognise yourself in Martha... ask God to make you more like Mary.

Action: Write down one thing you'll start changing from now.

Read Mark 10 v 17-23
- What does the man want? How does he think he can get it?
- What is stopping him from getting it? What is his idol?
- What does Jesus know about him? How does he deal with him?

Pray: If you understand exactly how the rich young man felt (v 22)... ask God to teach you the poverty of financial wealth, and the riches of total dependence on him.

Action: Write down one thing you will start changing from now.

Read Matthew 20 v 20-28
- What is the mother's priority for her sons? What does that say about her idol?
- What has she and the disciples missed?
- How does Jesus deal with them all?

Pray: If you dream of success and honour for yourself or your children... ask God to fill your heart and mind with Christ, his Son, yet your Servant, Sacrifice and Saviour.

Action: Write down one thing you will start changing from now.

Read John 4 v 7-19
- What do the woman's responses to Jesus tell us about her heart?
- How had the woman been trying to quench her thirst? What was her idol?
- How does Jesus deal with her?

Pray: If you struggle with discontent and disappointment in your relationships... ask God to help you turn from the dry wells of human relationships to Jesus Christ, the living water.

Action: Write down one thing you will start changing from now.

Read Matthew 26 v 6-13
- What does the Pharisee's knowledge of the woman lead to?
- What does Jesus' knowledge of the woman lead to?
- What's the outcome for the woman of Jesus' intimate knowledge of her?
- How might this woman sum up her new identity, do you think?

Pray: If you can't relate to this woman's unashamed love for Jesus... ask God to make you like her.

Action: Write down one thing you will start changing from now.

Jesus' intimate knowledge of us is not something to be afraid of and hide from.

In all of these encounters he gently encourages each individual to put their dependence and trust in him, rather than in these idols, which cannot deliver what they seem to offer.

Trying to find your identity in things of this world, be that money, relationships, status or happiness, will still leave you thirsting for more.

Jesus says: "Thirst for me. I am the one who offers you true life. Don't give your heart away to things that are temporary. I will give you eternity."

STEP
10

beauty

Why are TV programmes like *You are what you eat*, *How to look good naked* and *What not to wear* so successful?

It's because they play exactly to our insecurities about ourselves: they offer us "tailor-made" self-esteem; they know the buttons to push to keep us watching and spending money.

There's nothing wrong with wanting to look good, with nice clothes and money. There are positive examples of well-dressed, beautiful and rich women in the Bible (eg: Esther, Lydia, the wife of Proverbs 31).

The problem is when we take these good things from God and twist them into comfort idols – our priority, the thing we worship.

- How do you feel when someone pays you a compliment?
- Do you rely on clothes to give you confidence?
- Do you spend ages getting ready for certain people?
- Do you judge other people by what they're wearing?
- Do you have piles of clothes you never wear?

Often we buy clothes, accessories, or shoes because we believe they'll make us feel better about ourselves. But it doesn't last for long.

The source of our discontent is usually ourselves – especially our bodies. We're just trying to hide the flaws that we know too well.

Some of the most desperately unhappy and insecure women are shopaholics, caught in a downward spiral because none of their purchases will make them feel better about themselves.

Two things to think about:

1. The media image of beauty is in fact a lie.

Listen to Julian Hardyman:

"God loves variety. That's why we are all so different. There is huge variety in creation. But commercial interests prefer to standardize. So they can make money by exploiting the insecurities of the majority who don't fit the ideal pattern. Which they define and choose. And change when it suits them. So they decree that certain sizes and shapes are OK – while others are not." (Idols p. 65)

Magazine images ... what you see is not what you get.

Did you know the poster of Julia Roberts for *Pretty Woman* wasn't her? Her body was removed and someone else's substituted. Magazine images are routinely airbrushed. None of them is the real deal. What you see is not what you get.

2. True beauty is only found in Jesus.

Julian Hardyman again:

"The cross is an unlikely location to find beauty. But as we turn and fix our eyes on Jesus, we look away from the false cultural idols, breaking their power. What the cultural media images have destroyed in our imagination the cross can restore. The Son of God becoming sin for me restores [my vision] so that I can see what is truly beautiful.

This renewal of the imagination has the power to release us from the constant pressure to compare ourselves to the false image. It allows us to look in the mirror without shame. We will see beauty where we saw lack. We will see our naked faces reflecting the love of God." (Idols p. 71)

Reflect on Isaiah 53. What does it tell us about Jesus' physical beauty?

*t*estimony

It was the mid '90s and I was a teenager in Singapore, where it seemed that everyone looked, sounded, and dressed the same.

I wanted to stand out from the crowd, so I turned to fashion for the answer. I was part of a sub-culture known for scouring Japanese street-fashion magazines and rummaging in second-hand shops from Hong Kong to New York for the vintage wear we so valued.

An example of my "uniform" consisted of 3/4-length polyester skirt; men's traditional, Chinese silk, dragon-print top; 10-cm-high platform boots; 4-cm-long waxed-up hair; and cat-eye (lensless) glasses.

We took pride in the stares of onlookers and being photographed by European street-fashion reporters. What I wore and how I looked determined much of who I was, along with my taste in music, films, and art. Clearly, I took refuge in fashion and culture to set myself apart.

Sometimes I questioned my fashion uniqueness, especially when new trends so quickly became popular and established. But an encounter with a Christian friend was more destabilising.

I found her, and her community, attractive – not for how they looked (comfortable in their jeans and t-shirts) but because of their truthfulness, wisdom, and care for the outsider – me. I was struck by the curious joy of being what they described themselves to be – "children of God, beautiful and precious in his sight".

It pierced through the vanity parade that I and my friends were addicted to.

Knowing Christ and being clothed in his righteousness has led to a much-needed transformation in how I view myself and others. Building my identity on him, and not on how I look, has freed me from slavery to fashion trends. Now I can dress more for comfort than attention, and make friends with those who have different tastes.

I'm also now aware of the dangers of visual seduction and the temptation to make judgements based on what I see. There have been moments – like being attracted to a non-believer based on his looks, his tapered trousers or the house he designed... like feeling ashamed when seen hanging out with someone who looks "sloppy"... I need to confess and repent of these times, and remind myself that, unlike people, the Lord doesn't look on the outward appearance but on the heart.

Knowing Christ and being clothed in his righteousness has led to a much-needed transformation in how I view myself and others

I think it is natural, and even right, for Christians to care about the relationship between who we are and the judgments we make on form and beauty. But I still need reminders to be freed from the imprisoning gaze of others and the deceptive attractiveness of what I see.

The truth is that what we see is also passing away. The only firm foundation for each of our unique identities is in living out the reality of Christ's resurrection and the death of death – living in grace, faith, hope and joy ... before others, and ultimately, before the audience of only One.

STEP
11

relationships

Sometimes it may feel as if everybody in the world is in a relationship except for you. It makes you ask questions of yourself: What's wrong with me? Am I not attractive? Am I not loveable? Why am I the one that's still single?

Now my aim here is not to deal with the issues of singleness and marriage, good or bad, or to answer the question: Will I ever get married?

No, the aim here is to help you identify whether this is an idol. Is this an area where you look for worth and value and identity? And in that sense this is written just as much to women in relationships as to those who are not.

So what's the message of the world?

You are only valuable when someone else thinks that you are, when you have a bloke in tow (though it doesn't really matter who!).

The world idolises women like Angelina Jolie, in the "perfect" relationship with the "perfect" man. The world pities those who seem "unlucky in love", like Jennifer Aniston – those who seem to have been jilted or left on the shelf. This blogger seems to capture what most people are thinking:

"Deep down I think she symbolizes the way people look at singles – with a little bit of pity, a little bit of sympathy and a whole lot of questions – like, 'What's she doing wrong?'"

http://pop-ed.celebedge.ca/2011/06/Jennifer-aniston
-or-why-it-sucks-being-single-in-hollywood.html

Arghhhh! If that's the message we're getting about being single, no wonder it can make us feel worthless! It just fuels those kinds of questions that we ask ourselves anyway!

Could this be the idol you struggle with? Think about these questions:

- Do you find yourself often daydreaming about being married?
- Are you tempted to think this will solve all your problems?
- Is your sense of value in whether or not you are attracting the opposite sex?
- Do you rely on the fact that you've had relationships to make you feel better about yourself?

What about those of us in relationships?

How do we get it wrong? For many of us, our relationship with the man in our life gives us an awful lot of security, and we love to rely on that. We feel that we are needed and loved. But do we feed off that?

- Do you repeatedly ask your husband: "Do you love me? Do you want to be with me?"

Even if you're not verbalising it, is that how you feel inside? Relationships can bring out enormous amounts of insecurity in us, because they are so tied up with our identity.

We feel that if a man loves us we are worth more; whereas a poor relationship or no relationship means we are worth little.

- How does Psalm 139 give you a sense of God's love and care for you?
- How does that compare with the love of a man?

Finding identity in sex

This huge emphasis from the outside world on relationships has a vast amount to do with sex. *Are you having it? Are you getting enough of it? Is it good enough?* We are subtly blitzed with those kinds of questions when we watch romantic films, read magazines, see headlines etc. The message is: If you're not having sex, you're worthless. If sex is unsatisfying, then your partner is worthless.

Sex is always painted as the ultimate, romantic, fulfilling and satisfying experience, which, sadly, is far from the truth. By contrast, you rarely hear the truth about sex – that it can be awkward... it can be full of hurts and regrets... it won't always satisfy... that good sex takes time.

Think about this quote:

"Sex can give the illusion of identity. If you have several women, then you're a 'real man'. If you experience deep affection for a person of the same gender, then you must be a 'homosexual'. If you have not had sex with another person, then somehow you are 'incomplete'. These lies hinder deep friendships and prevent people from finding their true identity in Jesus.

Sex can give the illusion of intimacy. People long to be known and accepted. Sex will masquerade as real intimacy, making people superficially feel close to others without the time, effort and genuine love that real intimacy requires."

Dr Rod Woods, City Temple, FUTURE FIRST

> *Sex can give the illusion of identity ... sex can give the illusion of intimacy*

- **People use sex to define themselves. Are you in danger of doing the same? How?**

Don't believe the lie that you are defined by a biological function. Psalm 139 tells us that we are so much more than our sexuality.

You are fearfully and wonderfully made; you are intimately known by God; and everything that has, or has not, happened to you has been ordained by the good God who knows you better than you know yourself.

maid, mother or moneymaker?

*I'm a housewife ...
and I feel that
I'm just about the
least interesting
person in the room*

"What do you do?"

At the moment, it's the question I most dread, but it's impossible to avoid! We all ask it; it's how you get to know someone and start up a conversation. But have you ever thought what that question is saying about our identity? *"You are what you do."*

The reason why I dread this question is because of my answer: I'm a housewife, homemaker, domestic engineer, house-person... whatever the politically correct term is nowadays!

This seems to bring most conversations to an abrupt halt, and I feel that I'm just about the least interesting person in the room.

Feeling inferior

Actually I enjoy staying at home with my daughters, but I still feel I have to justify what I do. So I talk about what my job used to be, or that I'm studying part-time, or that I'm involved in different activities in church.

It's as if to say you're a homemaker is equal to saying: "I'm nothing! What I do is of no value or interest to anyone."

It's not just mothers and housewives who hate this question. How valuable would you feel having to tell people that you're a cleaner? How different would that be if you were a management consultant? What if you're unemployed?

There's nothing wrong with any of these, but do we judge others and ourselves by how far we've "moved up the career ladder"?

Hiding embarrassment

I recently met a man who cleaned ovens for a living. He spent the entire time telling me how he actually has several degrees... that he's a qualified engineer... that he had to leave his high-profile job for health reasons... So much detail! So many things to explain! He was clearly embarrassed by what he did!

Proving our "worth"

You see, the trap we fall into is finding our worth and value in what we do. And the real danger for women is that we find ourselves fighting to prove our worth and value in the area of work.

And that's when we end up looking down on those who don't earn money or use their time in a way that we think is "valuable".

Pop back to Genesis, and read about the first ever woman to be created:

Read Genesis 2 v 18-25
- Why did God make Eve?
- How did he go about it? What does that show us about her?
- What was Adam's response to Eve?

The high calling of "helper"

Perhaps as you read the word "helper", you picture Eve in an unflattering tabard, sporting the words *"Adam's little helper"*, waiting to be told by Adam what to do.

But that is not what is being described here. God himself is described as Israel's "helper". (See Isaiah 41, Psalm 33 v 20, 70 v 5 etc.) How can "helper" be a degrading term if it's used about the Lord himself?!

Complementing and completing men

What this passage tells us is that Adam needed Eve. Men need women. One Bible teacher jokingly puts it this way: "Men are incompetent – that's why God created women!" We are told in 1 Corinthians 11 v 7 that "woman is the glory of man"; that is, woman *completes* man. And not just in terms of marriage – men and women complete each other on a global scale.

How diminished the world would be if there was only one gender! God has already given women the supremely worthwhile role of helping, complementing and completing man; of *being women*, rather than trying to be more like men. But here comes our problem...

> *God has already given women the supremely worthwhile role ... of being women, rather than trying to be more like men*

Genesis 3 v 16b:
"Your desire will be for your husband, and he will rule over you." *(See Step 6, p16)*

The result of the fall means that we will always struggle with wanting the man's role. That's why we instinctively battle to prove our worth through work.

That is what we tell ourselves is valuable – not cleaning, cooking or bringing up children, but doing the "important" stuff, earning the dough. Work easily becomes an idol to us and we're duped into believing that without it we don't do anything of much value.

I see it in friends and I see it in myself: is it something that God is challenging you to change? Think about these questions:
- Do you find your identity in what you do?
- Do you look down on others because of what they do or don't do?
- What makes you feel this way?

Read Galatians 3 v 26-29
- What does this passage say about your identity in Christ?
- What role does gender play?
- What does it mean to be an heir? What will you inherit?
- How does it make you feel to be clothed in Christ?
- How can this make a difference to how you view your work in or outside the home?

*t*estimony   DIANE'S STORY

Am I that old?!

I remember realising I was being seen as a potential mother-in-law... catching sight of my arms in a mirror as I was going up an escalator... understanding those twinges were probably the onset of arthritis... realising my children would never live at home in the same way as they set off on their gap years.

People around me jokingly said: *"It's downhill from here on"*. But when you've given your life to family for 30 years and you're no longer needed in the same way... when you're aware of reducing strength... when you recognise that many things you'd dreamed of doing you probably never will, what then? What's my life about now? Who am I?

I've come to see that this stage of life is a wonderful opportunity. It's good to evaluate and face up to what I've been living for so far, and see that things the world tells me are important are things I can't keep hold of.

My appearance and health will show my age; my achievements will at best be things in the past; even my relationships will change.

As I look back, I see things God has done for which I should be hugely grateful. I also see many failures – yet, because of Jesus' death for me, they are forgiven and will never be held against me.

And I still have a wonderful opportunity to grow. My decreasing strength prompts me to learn to depend on Christ in new ways and grow

in my relationship with him. And he still has good works for me to do.

My family may not need me as much, but I can give that time to others for Jesus' sake. And the hope I have in Christ is so different from the expectations of those around me that it should make the gospel very attractive and prompt them to ask me the reason for the hope I have.

I know that life will always involve struggle. I live in a creation in bondage to decay, and I battle my sinful nature and Satan's temptations every day of my life. But in Christ I am secure. I am loved, forgiven and kept by God for eternity with him, beyond the best I can imagine.

I will have a resurrection body free from all decay. and will be free from the presence of sin to fully please and enjoy God for ever, in a perfectly restored creation, together with all who love Christ. And I'm getting closer to it every day!

The more I dwell on these things, the more I'm able to accept and even embrace my situation now, seeing it as God's wise way to make me more like Jesus

> *My decreasing strength prompts me to learn to depend on Christ in new ways and grow in my relationship with him*

and give me opportunities to point others to him. Paul put it this way:

"Therefore we do not lose heart. Though outwardly we are wasting away, yet inwardly we are being renewed day by day. For our light and momentary troubles are achieving for us an eternal glory that far outweighs them all. So we fix our eyes not on what is seen, but on what is unseen..."
(2 Corinthians 4 v 16-18)

STEP

13

who's in control?

One big identity struggle for women is in the area of control. It's important for us to look as if we're coping.

So, when we lose control in one area, we often compensate by being overly controlling elsewhere. For some that means an obsession with what we eat or how much we exercise. For others it can mean filling our diaries, so that we're never on our own and always appear busy and needed.

- How do you try and keep up the appearance of control?

Psalm 139 v 5, 10, 16

5 You hem me in—behind and before; you have laid your hand upon me.

10 even there your hand will guide me, your right hand will hold me fast.

16 All the days ordained for me were written in your book before one of them came to be.

- According to the psalm, who is in control?
- How is that a good thing?
- What do we need to do to give up the delusion that we're in control, do you think?

God is our Creator and Maker; he knows each of us intimately. There can be no one better to give control of our lives to.

Worry

Maybe I am being unfair on our sex here, but I think that not only are women instinctive controllers, we are also worriers.

The two things are inextricably linked. Since the fall, women have followed Eve in trying to prove themselves as better than men (see Step 12, p 30-31).

No doubt women tend to have certain qualities (like multi-tasking) which may make us better organised in certain areas. But it's the need to prove ourselves as better (than men, than other women) which truly explains why we are so confoundedly controlling. But what happens when we lose control? We worry.

"Will he do it properly?" "Will they do it the way I want it?" "Will it get done on time?"

Could this be why women take so much luggage on holiday, and new mums are weighed down like packhorses every time they leave the house? Something for every eventuality, just in case!

Distrust

Have you ever realised that worry is a sin? When we worry, we say to God: "I don't believe you when you say you're in control. That's simply not good enough. I need to be in control." Worry = refusing to trust God. As you read Psalm 139, do you see a God you can't trust? Surely not!

Delusion

Ask yourself: how much do you know about even your own innermost workings? Now compare God's intimate knowledge of us. But the psalm doesn't stop there.

God's presence, and therefore his power to intervene, is everywhere. And his plans – "all the days ordained for me" – are unstoppable. How deluded are we – and how wrong – to dare imagine we are better qualified to run our lives!

So chill out, sister! Your identity is not found in how much control you have in any situation. You cannot assume ultimate control: that is God's place and God's right, and we can rest assured that he knows what's best.

"How happy are they who can resign all to him, see his hand in every dispensation, and believe that he chooses better for them than they possibly could themselves!"

> # *When we worry, we say to God: "I don't believe you when you say you're in control"*

Three tips for building trust in God

1. Get to know God

The people we trust most are the ones we know best. You need to know someone's history, and see how they've been trustworthy with others, to begin trusting them yourself. God has given us his track-record in the Bible. We see that he is the Promise-Maker and Promise-Keeper. Reading about God's goodness, promises and faithfulness will help you trust him more and more.

2. Trust God every day

People who need to put total trust in someone – like the woman in the knife-throwing act – often start with small steps. Constant practice leads to spectacular trust. What starts as blunt knives thrown from a metre away ends up as flaming machetes hurled across a stage!

Talk to God about how hard you find it to trust him. Daily ask for his help and guidance in your everyday problems. Make a habit of these small steps of trust. Then, when a major crisis breaks, turning to God will more likely be your first resort, and not your last.

3. Remember what God has done

Many people have a searing childhood memory of someone who broke a promise. One event like this can spoil a relationship forever. God always keeps his promises. But we often forget his faithfulness.

Why not record answers to prayer and give thanks for them? Gather stories of what God has done in the lives of others. Most of all, remind yourself constantly of Jesus' death on the cross and what it means for you. Memorise Romans 8 v 32 and remember God's faithfulness every time you're tempted not to trust in God.

reflection & prayer

I recently watched the film *Confessions of a Shopaholic*. I know – but, honestly, it was all in the cause of research for this booklet!! In the film, the main character, Rebecca, ends up going along to "shopaholics anonymous".

But instead of being saved from her addiction, she ends up talking about the amazing feeling that shopping gives her and how much she loves it...

As a result the whole group rushes off to a sale to buy what they can.

So far we have looked at a number of identity comfort idols that women in particular are tempted to look to for a sense of worth.

But I don't want us to be like Rebecca – just paying lip-service to the fact that these idols are wrong; slipping back into the same old ways of life as soon as we put down this magazine.

We need to deal with our idols: to see the lies that they offer us, to think more deeply about ourselves and why we fall for them. So here are some questions to try and help you think through these things:

- What do I turn to for a sense of value, self-worth and identity?
- What is it that these things offer me? Why do I believe them?
- Where am I vulnerable to falling into this trap? (It could be a time of day, a particular place, a particular group of people.)
- How do these idols make me feel about myself in the short term and in the long term?
- Why do I need to find my value in these comfort idols? What do I not believe about God?

Read Isaiah 44 v 1-23

Prayer points:
In light of Isaiah 44, think of one thing...
- for which you can praise and thank God
- which you need to confess and change
- which you need to ask for God's help with.

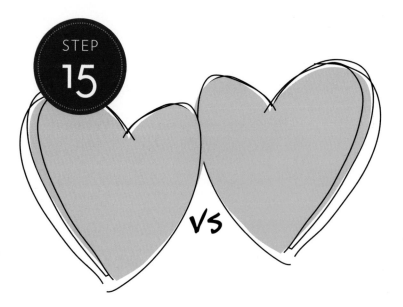

STEP

15

two hearts

66 There it was again: an all
too familiar voice ... that so
convincingly portrays me as
small, inadequate, undesirable,
insignificant. Why do I hate myself
so much sometimes?"
*(Anonymous woman quoted by Graham
Beynon in Mirror, mirror)*

Maybe you can imagine yourself saying
this. Here's someone in the grip of insecurity,
struggling to find their identity in what the
world sees as important, and ending up
feeling inferior and useless. We might be
tempted to respond with something like:
"Buck up, old girl. Don't be so down on yourself."
But astonishingly, there's oodles of truth
in her statement... When God looks at our
hearts, he does see something very small, very
inadequate and totally undesirable.

Romans 3 v 9-20
Read it again.
- What are your initial impressions of the
  human heart?
- What do you find most shocking in
  these verses?

The truth about us
The truth is, even on our good days we
are disgusting to God. Our best attempts
to please him are like offering him filthy rags

*Our "good deeds"
are nothing better
than a piece of old
chewing gum stuck
to the bottom of
a shoe*

(Isaiah 64 v 6). Our "good deeds" are nothing better than a piece of old chewing gum stuck to the bottom of a shoe. *"Here God, look at this. I did it for you!"*

Look again at the quote at the top. This person has been playing the comparison game – you know, the one where you look around you and either make yourself feel better (*"At least I don't look like that!"*) or worse (*"Why can't I ever be as good as that?"*) than others.

We all do it, and end up either with a dangerously high opinion of ourselves, or wallowing in self- pity.

Well, read Romans 3 again – no room for comparison games here. We all stand on a level playing field and this is the lowest of the low you can go. We are all worthless.

The advice of the world

What do you think a counsellor might say to the woman quoted at the top? What's the world's advice? *"Get yourself a good dose of self-esteem. Don't worry about what people think of you. It's what you think about yourself that matters. Be happy with who you are."*

....

Here's the worth God gives us: the death of His Son!

....

But the problem is: no amount of self-produced self-esteem is going to change the nature of our hearts. Yet the world can only urge us to look within ourselves for the solution, to bolster up our self-image, to tell ourselves: *"You're worth it"*.

Mostly, that's how we deal with insecurity. We go back to our comfort idols: buying new clothes, dieting, playing comparison games. Things that make us feel worth something for a while. But a close examination of my heart tells me that I'm not worth it – I'm worthless. No amount of self-help can change this situation – we need major outside help.

"BUT"...

Now read Romans 3 v 21-24

(**Righteousness** = having a clean, pure heart before God; being acceptable to him; no longer having to hide from him.)

* Write down everything you can from these verses about this righteousness, where it comes from and how it happens.

See the first word in v 21? I love these big "BUT"s in the Bible. Finally, here's a dose of real self-esteem:

> GOD has made YOU righteous!
> *Meaning?*
> You didn't have to do anything: GOD has made YOU righteous.
> *How?*
> Through Jesus... through the cross... through his blood.
> *Well, what do I have to do to get it? How can I ever pay him back?*
> Are you listening? It's free – read it again! JUSTIFIED FREELY (v 24). GOD has made YOU righteous... for FREE!

God's heart is not like ours. God's heart is full of GRACE. God doesn't measure whether or not we're up to scratch. He freely gives us what we don't deserve.

So don't go looking inside yourself for self-esteem. Here's the worth God gives us: the death of his Son! You can have what you simply do not deserve! No need to look for identity and comfort in the things around us. And no point! No possession, relationship, or status can do for us what God's done.

Whoredom

Remember Hosea? He was God's holy prophet, told to marry a prostitute, Gomer.

This symbolised how God's people had treated him, and highlighted the reality of their idolatry – turning to other gods was like selling themselves as whores. Gomer doesn't stick around for long. Before Hosea can blink she's back to her old ways. But here's how Hosea is told to treat her:

Hosea 3 v 1-3 (ESV)

1 And the LORD said to me, "Go again, love a woman who is loved by another man and is an adulteress, even as the LORD loves the children of Israel, though they turn to other gods and love cakes of raisins."

2 So I bought her for fifteen shekels of silver and a homer and a lethech of barley.

3 And I said to her, "You must dwell as mine for many days. You shall not play the whore, or belong to another man; so will I also be to you."

Imagine the humiliation of not just taking back your adulterous wife, but paying for her! But Hosea does this. Gomer gets what she truly doesn't deserve – a faithful, loving and forgiving husband. She has run after other men, and yet... she is shown grace.

What a stunning picture of God's gracious and compassionate heart to people like us, who always run to other things for comfort, security, value and identity. He is willing to buy us back, not just for a few shekels, but with the sacrifice of his Son.

You can have what you simply don't deserve

transformed identity

There are lots of changes in life that we may go through as women – changes in status and circumstances: teenager to adult, single to married, working to mother, mother to home-alone, mother to grandmother, wife to widow.

How we deal with these changes tells us a lot about where we find our identity. But the biggest change in status takes place for those who trust in Jesus. And this transformation took place at the cross of Christ – before any of us today were even a twinkle!

Colossians 1 v 21-23

- What is the status of people before they are transformed by the cross?
- How does that compare with the status of those who believe in the cross?
- What do these transformed people have to do?

New status

Verse 22 – here's another big Bible "BUT"! Through the cross, Jesus presents us to God as holy, without blemish and free from accusation.

- **"Holy"**: Completely pure and right with God. When he looks at his people he sees goodness, perfection, righteousness, holiness, godliness... Is that what you see when you look in the mirror? Not me! But that is what God now sees – true Christians are "holy in his sight".

- **"Without blemish"**: Nothing to do with our skin, or whether or not we've spilt gravy down our front. No, this is now the believer's character reference. There are no spots on our record, no guilty deeds staining our reputation, no indelible sins in our past, present or future. All those marks have been washed away, rubbed off, eradicated.

- **"Free from accusation"**: Before God, no one can point the finger at a Christian. No one can accuse us of anything that will again alienate us from him. There's nothing on our record, no sin, nothing!

Old lies

And yet, haven't you heard that little nagging voice? *"You know God doesn't really love you, not after what you've done. I'm not sure you can pray to God now; there's no way he's going to want to hear from you! And you haven't had a "quiet time" for over a week. What kind of a Christian do you call yourself?!"*

Who's accusing us like this? Sometimes we're speaking to ourselves, but sometimes it's the great accuser himself, Satan. He loves to put these doubts into our minds. *"God won't let you into his kingdom – you don't even belong in church. Who do you think you are?!"*

New verdict

Well, do you know what verse 22 says to those accusing voices? "SHUT UP!" There is nothing that you can be accused of: your sin has already been dealt with; you are no longer guilty. That is God's verdict on you!

There's only one thing required of us in these verses: don't stop believing! Hold on to the gospel. Don't move from it! Sounds simple, doesn't it? But the gospel may be one of the first things that a Christian forgets... that's what we're doing when we listen to the world and try and carve out a new identity for ourselves!

But here is your transformed identity! Here is how God sees you – HOLY, PURE, GUILT-FREE. This is what Jesus has made you. And there's more...

Read Colossians 3 v 1-4
- What are Christians told about their status here?
- What do those things mean? Try to put them in your own words.

Now or then?

At first glance these verses might seem a little confusing. Is Paul talking about the future? Or now? Well, the answer is both. He talks about the future as a present reality to teach us about our true identity in Christ now.

As a Christian, your life is now hidden with Christ. Our identity is so tied up with Jesus, so closely united with him, that right now our true lives are with him in glory, hidden with God.

"When Christ, who is your life, appears, then you also will appear with him in glory."

"Christ ... is your life." His righteousness, purity and godliness are yours and waiting in heaven with God now, to be revealed on that final day in glory and splendour. Hidden with Christ in God – that's where you belong now.

This is mind-blowing stuff! God has taken us (small, inadequate, undesirable) and given us this new identity in glory. This is GRACE.

True identity

Our future in heaven is so secure that it is a reality now. Although we can't yet see our heavenly reality, it is a true reality – more real than this earth and what we now appear to be.

This is who we Christians really are – spotless, holy, pure, already with Jesus, who we will be with for all eternity. Do you get this? The true you, the true me is already in heaven, already glorified.

And our future in heaven is so secure that we have nothing to fear as we come to God.

His grace means there's nothing we can do to make him love us any more – he already loves us as much as he loves his Son.

And there's nothing we can do to make God love us any less – he has already completely and totally eradicated our sin.

God's grace means we can always come to him – no matter how good or bad we feel, we can approach him with confidence. Grace means we can hold our heads up high, knowing our true identity is now with Jesus in heaven.

> *There's nothing we can do to make God love us any more ... and nothing we can do to make God love us any less*

becoming who you are

F or several years I worked with students for a well-known Christian organisation.

It was a great job and I enjoyed it very much, but when I became pregnant I knew I'd have to leave – working with students and looking after babies don't mix too well!

This was a massive struggle for me, because not only was I leaving a job I loved, but I felt I was somehow "downgrading". I felt as if I'd be reduced to toddler groups and inane conversations about nappy brands and breastfeeding.

For me it was a massive change in status and it seemed that I was no longer going to be important – valued or needed by other people.

Do you see the idols I was harbouring in my heart? Although I was doing "Christian work", so much of it was really about being recognised and boosting my own self-esteem.

That was where I was finding my identity, rather than in Jesus' love and what he's done for me.

Church service

Sadly, for many of us, even our service in the church can be motivated by the wrong reasons. Could this be true of you as well? Think about these questions:

- Do you only volunteer for those jobs that are up front and seen by others?
- Do you feel resentful at all towards those who have the up-front roles?
- Do you like to feel needed by others?
- Is your "generosity" really a way of you proving your value and worth?

If we've been serving in the church for years, we can become quite possessive over the roles we've been given. New ideas and small changes might make us feel angry and frustrated, or devalued and worthless. These are signs that we've been finding our identity in our roles and responsibilities.

In Colossians we have already looked at our transformed identity in Christ, but Paul goes on to describe the outward transformation that goes alongside our new identity.

This is not a set of rules for how a Christian should live and make themselves acceptable to God. No, this is a response to the inward change that Christ has already achieved in you. This is a Christian becoming who you already are in Jesus.

Read Colossians 3 v 1-17

- Put into your own words what characterises an earthly nature.
- Are any of these things evident in your heart?
- What reasons does Paul give why we should change?
- What characterises your new identity?

The "What not to wear" *of Christian living!*

Change of clothes

A friend once described this as the *"What not to wear"* of Christian living (Trinny and Susannah, eat your heart out!). Do you see why we're not to live like this any more?

This is what you used to be like (v 7). You've taken this stuff *off* (v 9); it simply doesn't suit you any more; you've outgrown it.

Can you imagine a church where we all actually "dressed" like God's chosen people? There would be no room for comparison, jealousy or resentment. Our hearts would be completely driven by loving and serving others, not proving our worth and gaining recognition for ourselves.

This is what a transformed identity in Christ looks like lived out. The key is in verse 1: *"Christ is all, and is in all"*.

If we are finding our self-esteem, worth, value and identity in Christ... if we are convinced that is where everyone else's identity should be found... then we are set free to love each other wholly and completely.

No more rivalry and comparison. No longer feeling superior or inferior. An end to constant belly-button gazing and looking within ourselves. Our motivation would no longer be the appreciation of others, but the good of others. What a witness! How countercultural! How Christlike!

- So, where have you been finding your identity in church?
- How do you need to change your thinking?

Prayer points:

In light of Colossians 3, think of one thing...
- for which you can praise and thank God
- which you need to confess and change
- which you need to ask for God's help with.

*t*estimony ANNE'S STORY

It was being ill with dysentery that led my heart to sing: *"O LORD, our Lord, how majestic is your name in all the earth"* (Psalm 8 v 1).

I'd become a Christian a few years earlier and was now training as a youth worker. I loved my job and loved being a Christian. I was keen as mustard, worked flat out late into the night and carried on my non-Christian personality of being successful at everything. I loved Jesus and, having been to the Philippines and seen God's heart for street children, I had high ambitions to be his hands to deprived children in the UK or abroad.

I visited some missionaries working in the slums in South America and came back with severe dysentery. I still led the youth weekend away and kicked off an evangelistic course I'd written but health problems meant I was signed off for a month – then another and another. A shower became the greatest thing I could achieve in a day (and I had to sleep for two hours to recover).

Everything about my Christian life was taken away. I went from leading a weekend away to going on a houseparty and spending most of it in bed; from running an evangelistic course to struggling to even pray for it; and from being a good listener to battling to sit up if friends came round. I even struggled to read a verse from the Bible.

I wasn't sure of God's love and felt utterly worthless. I was giving nothing to God and doing nothing for him. I felt so far from him and like a failed Christian. Driven by this feeling of worthlessness I kept trying to work and meet with people but would then crash even further into fatigue. Then two things happened that brought me to the true view of God and therefore myself.

On one of my better days I heard from my missionary friends. They 'd included me in a prayer letter and an American sent them this email: "Tell your friend that God wants her to know he loves her very much". That's true: Jesus' death on the cross tells me so. This email made me realise God loved me regardless of what I did and didn't do.

That was when I experienced God's grace in a new way. I saw my relationship with him had been centred on my achievements. So when I couldn't do anything for God, I felt unloved by him and worthless. I was robbing Christ of the praise he deserved for the victory he'd won and the status he'd already given to me.

God continued to wow me with how gloriously he deals with us. I was moving church and needed to raise funds myself. But my fatigue stopped me doing this and I thought I'd have to put my life on hold. God in his grace moved someone to give me £5000 towards my next year. It was over half the amount I needed. I still don't know who did that but I'm thankful as it meant my praise went to God.

When I saw the cheque, I was breathless. I couldn't believe God had looked after me so wonderfully. He is awesome and mighty – but so gracious and caring in showing he had my life in his hands.

When things are going well and we can do things and achieve lots, we forget that God graciously gives everything to us through Christ's work. This robs us of praising Jesus, being overwhelmed by God's goodness and having full satisfaction in him alone.

I'm so pleased God gave me the opportunity to have my abilities taken away so that I could see it's because of his glory that he chooses and loves me, and nothing else.

I'm now well but I'm still in grave danger of thinking my standing with God revolves round me. We looked at Psalm 8 recently in our women's group and I was reminded again that Jesus is the centre of the universe. Life is at its best when he is.

the tricky bit

Back to Psalm 139. Now for the tricky bit! Why does David have to go and spoil a beautiful and poetic psalm by sticking in verses 19-22?

The "slay the wicked" passage comes as a bit of a jolt – what on earth is it doing here?

Psalm 139 v 19-22

¹⁹ If only you would slay the wicked, O God!
   Away from me, you bloodthirsty men!

²⁰ They speak of you with evil intent;
   your adversaries misuse your name.

²¹ Do I not hate those who hate you, O LORD,
   and abhor those who rise up against you?

²² I have nothing but hatred for them;
   I count them my enemies.

• Why do we find this passage so difficult? What are the bits you are uncomfortable with?

The whole picture

I guess these verses don't seem to fit with the picture we like to have of God, and the picture that has indeed been painted throughout the rest of the psalm.

God as our loving, caring, protective Creator... the gentle hand that guides us and holds onto us... the intimate knowledge of us and our inner workings...

But let's not distort the picture of God that the Bible gives. Yes, he is indeed a loving God, but he loves what is good and will not tolerate what is evil. It's not because he is impatient or intolerant in a human sense, but because he is blazing with purity, holiness and righteousness. Evil is simply not compatible with his nature; it is completely foreign to him.

Read verses 17 and 18 again.

> **17** How precious to me are your thoughts, O God! How vast is the sum of them!
>
> **18** Were I to count them, they would outnumber the grains of sand.
>
> When I awake, I am still with you.

- How does the psalm writer feel about God's thoughts?

Like God

We cannot possibly understand the mind of God, but we can have confidence in his sovereignty and goodness and grace.

If we truly belong to God, it means we must share in his heart – we must hate what he hates and love what he loves. That means hating sin, hating things that are opposed to God and God's way of living.

Unlike the world

"Hate" – it's strong, isn't it? In some ways, we live in a very tolerant society. I wonder if, all too easily, that tolerance creeps into our lives, and we become increasingly comfortable with things God wants us to hate. When that happens, our identity becomes merged with the world around us. There is no longer any distinction between us and the world.

Think about the kinds of TV programmes you watch, the magazines you read, the conversations you join in with. Is there anything in them you think God would hate?

Now listen, I'm not telling you to cut yourself off from the world around you and become a nun! But think about the strength of language that the writer uses here – hate, slay, away from me.

Is that how we feel about the things of this world? Just think about when you recommend a film or a book to a Christian friend. Does it go something like this: *"It has got this one dodgy part but most of it's ok"*? We're already making excuses for what we know God would hate! And yet we comfortably sit down to watch or read it!

The whole of God's word

People today, if they truly knew and understood God's word, would doubtless be shocked by some of the things it says. But then they come from the world, which stands in opposition to God and all he says and values.

But what about the loved, saved, forgiven people of God? Maybe the most shocking thing is that we are shocked by a passage like this in the psalm. David was God's king, his chosen and anointed one. He knew what it was to have God's heart: to be passionate about the things God loved, and opposed to the things God will not tolerate.

Surely we could take a leaf out of his book.

Psalm 139 is not the only part of God's word to make strong statements and call us to radical, countercultural, uncomfortable ways of living. Think about these other passages. What do they teach us about what we are to love and hate?

> **Proverbs 6 v 16-17; 8 v 13**
>
> **Luke 6 v 27-31**
>
> **Mark 8 v 34-38**

How closely is your identity tied in with this world? Do people know you are a Christian? If no, can they at least see that you are different from other people? If yes, do they see in you what kind of person a Christian should be?

Pray that you would be able to say to God: *"'How precious to me are your thoughts, O God!' – all of them!"*

> *If we truly belong to God … we must hate what he hates and love what he loves.*

STEP
19

audience of one

The other day I was getting ready to go and visit a friend of mine. But I had to go through several changes of clothes before I felt comfortable. Why?

Because she has more money and better taste than me. I didn't want to look like her poor frumpy friend! We've been friends for years, but there is still that inbuilt "woman thing" inside me about keeping up appearances, even with someone I'm close to.

Our audience

As I've been thinking through the whole issue of identity, it's struck me that so much of our struggle is because we give too much importance to what other people think of us.

But it's not just a matter of wanting to keep up appearances. It's also about wanting to fit in, to be accepted, liked and loved.

2 Timothy is probably the final letter that Paul wrote, and it speaks of people deserting him, abandoning him and hurting him (see, for

We give too much importance to what other people think of us

example, 2 Timothy 1 v 15; 4 v 10, 14, 16). But his instructions to Timothy are not: *"Try and fit back in again. See if you can try and make friends with those people. Win them over and make friends."* No, his instructions are clear: Timothy has an audience of One.

"Do your best to present yourself to God as one approved, a workman who does not need to be ashamed..." **2 Timothy 2 v 15**

Now, this instruction isn't just for Timothy and church leaders like him, but to all who have been transformed by the cross and given this new identity in Christ.

Is that you? Who, then, is your audience?

Read through Psalm 139 again.
- How do you feel about having God as your audience?
- What things are good about having God as an audience?
- What things are bad?

With God as my audience, I don't have to pretend or hide. He knows it all anyway.

I don't have to make excuses for who I am – for my looks or personality. He tenderly knit them together for me. But he also knows the bad as well as the good. He looks straight through the "holy" exterior that I show to others, and sees my sin for what it really is.

Our response

That's why this psalm ends with a response. The writer, understanding God's intimate knowledge of us, comes to God in repentance and longing to change. Wanting to be even more fully known, if that were possible.

But perhaps this response is also about us coming to know more about ourselves; asking God to dig deeper and show us our hidden flaws.

Psalm 139 v 23-24

23 Search me, O God, and know my heart; test me and know my anxious thoughts.

24 See if there is any offensive way in me, and lead me in the way everlasting.

- What exactly does the writer want God to search out?
- How does that make you feel?
- What assurances do these verses give?

Why should we want our hidden flaws to be revealed to us? So that God, by rooting them out, can lead us in "the way everlasting".

It feels a bit "yuck", doesn't it, asking God to root out all the offensive stuff? But remember that as we come to him with our ugly, unimpressive and undesirable heart, he is the one who has already transformed us by the cross of Christ.

"The cross is where we find our security and our identity and our joy... the cross is where we find acceptance and forgiveness. The cross is where we find freedom from the compulsive need to please others. It's where we find the freedom to please God instead." (Julian Hardyman, *Idols* p. 70)

Our hope

The cross is where we are given our new identity, but it's also where we find our future hope – "the way everlasting". So I want to leave you thinking about your future identity. We've already come across it in Colossians 3 v 1-4 – have a read of those verses again.

Then read these verses from Revelation:

Revelation 19 v 6-9

6 Then I heard what sounded like a great multitude, like the roar of rushing waters and like loud peals of thunder, shouting: "Hallelujah! For our Lord God Almighty reigns.

7 Let us rejoice and be glad and give him glory! For the wedding of the Lamb has come, and his bride has made herself ready.

8 Fine linen, bright and clean, was given her to wear. (Fine linen stands for the righteous acts of the saints.)

9 Then the angel said to me, "Write: 'Blessed are those who are invited to the wedding supper of the Lamb!'" And he added, "These are the true words of God."

- What promises can you claim about your new identity?
- Who are you?
- What will you be wearing?!

This is your new identity. This is what you will be wearing. This is what you are preparing for.

What a wedding chorus!

What a transformation!

What an identity!

The cross is where we find our security and our identity and our joy ... acceptance and forgiveness ... freedom from the compulsive need to please others ... freedom to please God instead